Jobs if You Like...

Reading and Writing

Charlotte Guillain

Heinemann
LIBRARY
Chicago, Illinois

H **www.capstonepub.com**
Visit our website to find out more information about Heinemann-Raintree books.

To order:
☎ Phone 800-747-4992
🖱 Visit www.capstonepub.com to browse our catalog and order online.

Edited by Rebecca Rissman, Daniel Nunn, and Adrian Vigliano
Designed by Steve Mead
Picture research by Elizabeth Alexander
Originated by Capstone Global Library
Printed and bound in China by South China Printing Company

16 15 14 13 12
10 9 8 7 6 5 4 3 2 1

Library of Congress Cataloging-in-Publication Data
Guillain, Charlotte.
  Reading and writing / Charlotte Guillain.
    p. cm.—(Jobs for Kids Who Like...)
  Includes bibliographical references and index.
  ISBN 978-1-4329-6810-6—ISBN 978-1-4329-6821-2 (pb)
1. Book reviewing—Vocational guidance—Juvenile literature. 2. Book industries and trade—Vocational guidance—Juvenile literature. 3. Information science—Vocational guidance—Juvenile literature. 4. Library science—Vocational guidance—Juvenile literature. 5. Authorship—Vocational guidance—Juvenile literature. 6. Research—Vocational guidance—Juvenile literature. I. Title.
  Z471.G85 2012
  028.1023—dc23   2011031930

Acknowledgments
We would like to thank the following for permission to reproduce photographs: © Capstone Global Library pp. 10, 11, 18 (Lord and Leverett); Alamy pp. 13 (© Blend Images), 23 (© Jeff Morgan 14), 26 (© Geraint Lewis); Corbis pp. 14 (© Radius Images), 17 (© Stefanie Grewel/cultura), 19 (© Gideon Mendel), 22 (© Karen Kasmauski); Getty Images pp. 5 (© 2011 Akiko Aoki), 12 (Gary Gershoff/WireImage for Jumpstart for Young Children); Glow Images pp. 15 (Rubberball), 20 (Hill Street Studios/Blend Images), 21 (Caspar Benson/Fstop), 24 (JGI/Jamie Grill/Blend Images), 25 (Ghislain & Marie David de Lossy/Cultura); Photolibrary pp. 4 (Stoelwinder Stoelwinder/Bios), 6 (Das Fotoarchiv), 7 (Mohamad Itani), 9 (Comstock/White); Shutterstock pp. 8 (© Rob Marmion), 16 (© StockLite), 27 (© Robert Kneschke).

Cover photo of students rehearsing onstage reproduced with permission of Glow Images (Hill Street Studios/Blend Images).

Every effort has been made to contact copyright holders of material reproduced in this book. Any omissions will be rectified in subsequent printings if notice is given to the publisher.

Contents

Some words are shown in bold, **like this**. You can find out what they mean by looking in the glossary.

Why Do Reading and Writing Matter?

Do you think reading and writing are just for school? You couldn't be more wrong! You are reading all day long, probably without even realizing it! You read signs, instructions on computer games, captions on television, and many other things.

We need to read to find our way around.

You also need to write all the time to send e-mails, write shopping lists, and do your schoolwork. Read this book to find out about some great jobs that use reading and writing. Could one of them be for you?

Many people enjoy reading stories.

Be a Journalist

If you were a journalist, you would spend a lot of time reading and writing. Your job would be to find news stories and write about them for newspapers, television, the Internet, or radio. You would need to read a lot of information as you gather the facts for a story.

Journalists can travel all over the world.

Journalists need to check that all the facts they have collected are correct. Then they have to write the news story quickly and in a way people will understand.

Journalists have to go out and talk to people.

Be a Librarian

If you like reading, then you probably use a library. Librarians work in libraries, helping people to find the books or information they need. Their job is to organize all the **resources** in a library, including books, music, and electronic materials.

Librarians know where to find information.

Librarians give people advice on what to read.

Librarians use computers to organize and find information. Some librarians know a lot about one subject, such as history or science. Other librarians talk to children about reading and help them find books they enjoy.

9

Be an Editor

If you were an editor, you would work on new books or Websites. You would do a lot of reading as you check **manuscripts**. You would have to think carefully about who reads the book or Website, and what the writing should be like.

Editors check carefully to make sure that all of the details in a piece of writing are correct.

Editors read what an author has written and suggest ways to improve the final product.

Some editors find **authors** and help them to write text that readers will like. Other editors go through the text carefully and make sure there are no mistakes. Web editors have to make sure that the text on a Website is easy to read on a screen.

Be a Writer

There are many different things a writer can do! Some writers write stories or poems, and others write television programs or film **scripts**. Other writers write advertisements or Websites.

Many writers visit schools and libraries to read their books.

Writers need to be good at working with a **deadline**.

All writers need to spend time writing a first **draft** of their ideas. Then they might work with an editor before **revising** their writing. Writers need to be good at working on their own.

Be a Lawyer

If you were a lawyer, you would give people advice about the **law**. You would spend a lot of time reading about the law. You would need to know what the facts are and help explain them to people.

Lawyers are good at giving people the information they need.

Some lawyers have to write important documents, such as **contracts**. They might help people decide what they can and can't do. Other lawyers help people when they have to go to **court**.

Some lawyers have to present information and ask questions in court.

Be a Web Content Manager

If you like reading information on the Internet, then maybe you could be a web content manager. Your job would be to make sure all the information on a Website is correct. You would also need to think about who uses the Website.

Web content managers make sure people can read the information on their Websites easily.

Web content managers have to work with a team of people to solve any **technical** problems.

Web content managers need to make sure their Website is up to date. They might have to organize passwords for people to use the Website or arrange for things to be sold on the Website.

17

Be a Translator

If you were a translator, you would read text in one language and change it into another language. You might **translate** reports, documents, books, or Websites.

Translators need to be able to read and write in at least two languages.

Translators help people tell their stories to many other people.

Translators need to be able to translate writing so that it is correct and is in the right **style**. Sometimes they might need to know **technical** language. Often they have to work with a **deadline**.

Be an Actor

If you were an actor, you would do a lot of reading. You would have to read and learn your lines, or words, in a **script**. Then you would rehearse with other actors for a play, film, or television program.

Actors spend a lot of time reading scripts.

When actors perform, they have to remember their lines. They need to work well with other people and have plenty of energy. Some actors also work on the radio, in advertisements, or in schools.

Actors have to work well in a team with many other people.

Be a Bookseller

If you love reading, then imagine a job where you are surrounded by books every day! If you were a bookseller, you would buy books and sell them to people. You might sell all types of books or **specialize** in one type of book.

Some booksellers specialize in rare, old types of books.

Booksellers
organize events
such as
author visits.

Good booksellers give their customers advice on
which books to read. They read a lot of books
themselves to find out what they are about.
Sometimes **authors** visit their store and they
organize **book signings**.

Be a Public Relations Officer

If you were a public relations officer, your job would be to tell people about your **clients**. You would want people to like your clients and become their customers. You would work hard to let people know why your clients are good.

Public relations officers are good at talking to people.

Public relations officers have to write **brochures**, information for journalists, and Websites. They have to be very good at writing clear information. They also have to get along with many different people.

Public relations officers often read a lot of information and then share it with others.

Choosing the Right Job for You

When you decide what you want to do when you grow up, don't just think about school subjects. Think about what you enjoy doing. If you like to work on your own, then you might not want to be an actor!

If you love books, then you might like to be a librarian or bookseller. Nearly every job uses some reading and writing, so there should be something to suit everyone.

Five things you couldn't do without reading and writing

- Find your way around a new place
- Enjoy stories
- Learn information
- Know what to buy
- Order food at a restaurant

Reading and Writing Job Chart

If you want to find out more about any of the jobs in this book, start here:

	Actor	Bookseller	Editor	Journalist	
You need to:	Have a good memory	Love books	Be good at spotting spelling mistakes	Be a good writer	
Best thing about it:	When the audience claps!	Reading lots of books!	Seeing a finished book or Website!	Getting a headline story!	

Lawyer	Librarian	Public relations officer	Translator	Web content manager	Writer
Be good at reading a lot of information	Be good at using computers	Be able to write clearly	Be good at foreign languages	Be very organized	Be good at working on your own
Helping people win in **court**!	Helping people find the information they need!	Hearing good news about your company!	Helping people in another country understand something!	Seeing the finished Website!	Watching people enjoy your writing!

Glossary

author writer

book signing event when a writer signs copies of his or her books

brochure small booklet or magazine

client person who pays another person to work for them

contract legal agreement

court place where problems involving the law are solved

deadline date and time by which a job needs to be done

draft first, rough piece of writing

law set of rules that people must follow

manuscript piece of writing presented by an author

resource source of information

revise go over something again and make changes to make it better

script words that are spoken in a play, film, or television program

specialize focus on one particular area

style way in which something is written or done

technical to do with special skills and knowledge

translate change into words from another language

Find Out More

American Library Association
www.ala.org/ala/educationcareers/careers/
librarycareerssite/kids.cfm
This Website of the American Library Association
tells you what to do if you would like to be a
librarian someday.

Translator Career
www.bls.gov/oco/ocos175.htm
You'll find more information about what it takes to
be a translator at this Website. Have an adult help
you if you don't understand any of the information.

Law for Kids
www.lawforkids.org/
Interested in becoming a lawyer? Find out more
information about the law on this Website. You can
find out what legal terms mean and learn about
the legal documents of the United States.

Index